D0983405

ANCIENT CULTURES AND CIVILIZATIONS

THE CULTURE OF
SPARTA

Vic Kovacs

PowerKiDS
press™

NEW YORK

Published in 2017 by **The Rosen Publishing Group, Inc.**
29 East 21st Street, New York, NY 10010

Cataloging-in-Publication Data

Names: Kovacs, Vic.
Title: The culture of Sparta / Vic Kovacs.
Description: New York : PowerKids Press, 2017. | Series: Ancient cultures and civilizations | Includes index.
Identifiers: ISBN 9781508150053 (pbk.) | ISBN 9781499422603 (library bound) | ISBN 9781508149910 (6 pack)
Subjects: LCSH: Sparta (Extinct city)--History--Juvenile literature. | Sparta (Extinct city)--History, Military--
    Juvenile literature.
Classification: LCC DF261.S8 K68 2017 | DDC 938'.9--d23

Developed and produced for Rosen by BlueAppleWorks Inc.

Art Director: Haley Harasymiw
Managing Editor for BlueAppleWorks: Melissa McClellan
Editors: Janice Dyer, Marcia Abramson
Design: T.J. Choleva

Picture credits: p. 5 Renata Sedmakova/Shutterstock; p. 9 Leo von Klenze/Public Domain; p. 11 Ververidis
Vasilis/Shutterstock; p. 12 left GFDL/Creative Commons; p. 12 middle, 12 right john antoni/Creative
Commons; p. 13, 14 ©Twentieth Century Fox Film Corporation/ Photofest Digital Library; p. 15 Anastasios71/
Shutterstock; p. 17 Marie-Lan Nguyen/Public Domain; p. 18, 20 Jastrow/Public Domain; p. 19 Steff/Public
Domain; p. 23 top Dimitrios/Shutterstock; p. 23 bottom Shiler/Shutterstock; p. 24 Marie-Lan Nguyen/Creative
Commons; p. 27 Isaac Walraven/Public Domain; p. 28 siete_vidas/Shutterstock; p. 29 KLS/Public Domain;
Maps: p. 7 T.J. Choleva/Shutterstock: AridOcean; p. 8 T.J. Choleva/Shutterstock: Alfonso de Tomas

Manufactured in the United States of America
CPSIA Compliance Information: Batch #BS16PK: For Further Information contact Rosen Publishing, New York, New York at 1-800-237-9932

CONTENTS

CHAPTER 1

ANCIENT SPARTA

Sparta, also known as Lacedaemon, was a **city-state** in ancient **Greece** in the southern part of the country known as the Peloponnese. The large **peninsula** of Peloponnese was located southeast of Athens, which was Sparta's chief rival throughout their history. Though its history stretches all the way back to the **Neolithic** period, the society known as "Spartan" first began to take shape in the eighth century B.C.

The main region of the Spartan state was Laconia. Spartans began to successfully conquer their neighbors to the west in an area called Messenia. The Spartans enslaved the defeated Messenians, and forced them to do the manual labor, such as farming, that was necessary to maintain a society. Because they didn't need to concentrate on these everyday tasks, Spartans had the time to develop a culture focused completely on **military** ability. Their single-minded devotion allowed Sparta to become the leading military power in ancient Greece.

This extreme reliance on a slave class created repeated problems for Sparta in the form of rebellions, uprisings, and wars. However, Sparta became a legend through the centuries because of its incredible ability on the battlefield.

Lycurgus, c. 900–800 B.C., was a legendary lawmaker in Sparta. His laws focused on equality, military fitness, and living in a simple and plain way.

CHAPTER 2

PELOPONNESIAN WAR

By the sixth century B.C., Sparta was one of the most important and powerful city-states in ancient Greece. This influence only grew after the Peloponnesian League was formed. The League was an **alliance** between Sparta and many of its neighbor states. Other member states included Corinth, Tegea, and Elis. The only notable holdout on the peninsula was Argos, a rival of Sparta.

Unlike in the Delian League, formed in 478 B.C. and headed by Athens, members did not have to pay to join. They only needed to send a percentage of their troops when called on by Sparta. On the other hand, the League made sure that none of Sparta's neighbors would help the enslaved Messenians its society relied on. Sparta could even call on members of the League to help crush any slave uprisings.

KEEPING HELOTS IN CHECK

Part of the reason Sparta created the Peloponnesian League was so they would have allies willing to help them if the Messenian slaves, called helots, decided to revolt. This was important to them, as full Spartan citizens were greatly outnumbered by helot slaves.

Groups of villages in ancient Greece formed city-states for protection and to organize trade. Each Greek city-state had its own government, army, and territory to defend. However, they all spoke the same language, believed in the same gods, and thought of themselves as Greeks.

Thebes

Corinth

Elis

Argos

Tegea

Messenia

Sparta

Laconia

In the first half of the fifth century B.C., the **Persian Empire** invaded Greece. In order to defeat the massive outside army, Spartans and Athenians joined forces. By 479 B.C. the Greeks had repelled the invasion, and by 449 B.C. the Persians had agreed to a formal peace treaty. This period is known as the Greco-Persian War.

However, without a common enemy, relations between Sparta and Athens quickly soured. Sparta was alarmed at how much power and influence Athens was gaining. By the end of the Greco-Persian War, Athens was quickly becoming an empire. This buildup of territory and power, combined with rising tensions due to many smaller disagreements, would lead to the outbreak of the Great Peloponnesian War, beginning in 431 B.C.

The Peloponnesian League
- Sparta and its allies
- Athens and its allies
- Neutral states

Black Sea

Ancient Greece

Adriatic Sea

Italy

Persian Empire

Aegean Sea

Sicily

Athens was a powerful and influential city. It was so well-respected that the Spartans refused to destroy the city or enslave its citizens when Athens was defeated in the Peloponnesian War.

Though Sparta had the better army, Athens had a much larger navy. As a result, the war became long and brutal. Athens's and Sparta's allies fought the war as well. The war lasted until 404 B.C.

One major factor that led to Sparta's victory was a terrible plague that devastated Athens. Coming early in the war, in the year 430 B.C., it killed about a third of the entire Athenian population. By the end of the war, the entire country of Greece had become involved. Sparta even accepted help from its old enemies, the Persians. When Athens finally surrendered, it was a shadow of its former self, and would never truly recover. Sparta, as the victor, took its place as the dominant city-state in Greece.

CHAPTER 3

SPARTAN WAR MACHINE

Unlike Athens, which was famous for its **democracy**, Sparta was ruled by two kings. Each king was the head of one of two royal families, the Agiads and the Eurypontids. In times of war, one king would ride with and lead the army, while the other would remain in Sparta and rule the city.

Although these kings were the heads of Spartan society, they were not all-powerful. They were advised by five elected men, called the ephors, as well as a council of 28 elders, called the gerousia. Ephors were elected for a single year, and could not be elected again after serving. Members of the gerousia were members for life. Both groups were made up of men over the age of sixty. Both were elected by the assembly, which was made up of all Spartan citizens. These three tiers of government created a system in which it was almost impossible for one person or group to achieve total control of Sparta.

Spartan society was divided into three main social classes: Spartans, helots, and perioeci. The ruling class, Spartans, were the smallest in number. They were vastly outnumbered by their slaves, the helots. Perioeci weren't full citizens, like Spartans, but also weren't slaves, like helots. They had limited freedom and had to serve Sparta's interests.

Spartans took part in military drills from an early age. They were trained to honor the warrior society. As a result, Spartans were one of the most feared military forces in ancient Greece.

FEARLESS WARRIORS

When a Spartan boy turned seven, he was taken from his home and placed in the agoge, a military education system. A bit like a boot camp, boys were trained to be soldiers in both body and mind. After graduating, at age twenty, they began their full military service, which lasted until they were sixty. As a **hoplite**, all of their time was devoted to becoming a better and better soldier. Though they were encouraged to marry, they would still live in barracks with their fellow soldiers until the age of thirty.

In battle, soldiers wore red robes and bronze armor, including a helmet. Their main weapon was the dory, a type of spear. They also carried a shield, which was very important in Spartan culture. To lose a shield in battle was considered incredibly shameful. It's said that mothers would send their sons to battle by telling them, "Come back with your shield, or on it!" This shows that even Spartan mothers would rather have a son who died bravely in battle, than one who lived through the shame of losing his shield.

Spartan hoplites wore helmets and armor and carried shields and spears. Many of these items are on display in museums around the world.

The Spartans painted the Greek letter lambda on their shields. This symbol, which looks like an upside-down V, stood for Lacedaemon or Laconia.

The Spartan army fought using the phalanx formation. In a phalanx, soldiers group themselves together in lines, forming a rectangle. They then lock their shields together, and place their spears in front of the first row of shields. This made it very hard to break past the first row of hoplites, especially without injury. This was also why it was so unacceptable for a soldier to lose his shield: it left not just the loser vulnerable, but the entire formation. Although other Greek armies used the phalanx formation, Sparta's was seen as the best.

The core of the Spartan army was the hoplite. These extremely well-trained and disciplined foot soldiers made up the fearsome phalanx. Generally, only Spartan citizens were hoplites, and one could only gain citizenship by becoming a hoplite. Helots and perioeci also served in the military, but in much lesser roles. Perioeci were used in a lesser **infantry**, while helots generally helped their Spartan masters.

The Spartan method of war was mostly focused on ground combat. This was because Sparta was landlocked. While it was agreed that they had the strongest ground forces in all of Greece, they never developed an impressive navy.

BATTLE OF THERMOPYLAE

One incident that shows how the Spartans viewed warfare was the Battle of Thermopylae. During the Greco-Persian War, in August of 480 B.C., the decision was made to defend a mountain pass in northern Greece from Persian invaders. King Leonidas of Sparta led the combined Greek forces. With an army of just 7,000 Greeks, he managed to hold off a Persian force of between 100,000 and 150,000 for two full days.

Sparta had the strongest military in ancient Greece. It was considered the leader of the combined Greek forces during the Greco-Persian War.

FIGHTING PERSIANS

During the Greco-Persian War, Greece agreed to combine all its forces against the outside threat of the Persians. Sparta, widely known as the best military force in the country, was given command of this united army. Again and again, in the face of vastly superior numbers, the Greek forces were able to triumph, thanks to Sparta's leadership and excellence in battle. In many battles, Spartan soldiers led the charge, both to scare the enemy and inspire their fellow Greeks!

On the third day, Leonidas learned that a local Greek had betrayed them by showing the Persians a path that would lead behind the Greek battle lines. Knowing that defeat was now almost certain, Leonidas ordered most of his troops away. However, someone would have to stay to fight to give the Greeks time to retreat. Leonidas volunteered himself and 300 of his Spartans, along with about 1,100 other Greek soldiers. Looking certain death in the face, the Spartans fought down to the last man. None, including Leonidas, would survive, but the legend of the last stand of the 300 Spartans at Thermopylae would live on forever.

Although King Leonidas lost the Battle of Thermopylae, his death is seen as a heroic sacrifice. He was worshipped as a hero and shrines and statues were built in his honor.

CHAPTER 4

LIFE IN SPARTA

In Sparta, the state was the focus of life. It demanded total loyalty, and set out rigid guidelines for how people could live so they could best serve it.

FAMILY LIFE

Boys lived with their families until the age of seven. At that point, they were removed from their homes to start their education. Boys were taken to the agoge, where they were molded into the soldiers they would be for the rest of their lives. Male Spartans were allowed one job: hoplite, or soldier. Their active military service lasted until the age of sixty, when they were eligible to be elected to political office. Even after turning sixty, though, many men chose to continue to serve in the military.

Girls were allowed to continue to live with their families after the age of seven, though they still received a state-sponsored education. They tended to marry beginning at age eighteen, which was very late compared to women elsewhere in Greece.

TOUGH SCHOOL RULES

In the agoge, boys were encouraged to steal extra food, if they could. It was thought this would help them learn how to move secretly and quietly, skills that would help them in the military. However, if caught, they were punished with floggings.

Pottery found in archaeological digs shows images of everyday life in ancient Greece.

In fact, Spartan women generally had more freedoms than women elsewhere in the country. Not only were they educated, they were also not forced to worry about the manual labor that went into maintaining a household, like weaving and cooking. This was the job of the helots. As a result, women had more time to oversee the running of the household, including the agriculture. This meant women were basically responsible for the entire household's finances. They were also able to inherit property.

Though they were unable to vote, women often voiced their opinions and influenced their husbands. The greatest honor for a Spartan woman was to give birth to a fierce warrior, therefore much of their lives were focused on having as many healthy, strong babies as possible. Many in ancient Greece believed Sparta was actually run by women.

Spartan women worshipped individuals from Greek myths, such as Helen of Troy. She was considered the most beautiful woman in the world. A shrine to Helen of Troy was located in the center of Sparta.

Helots were slaves who worked mostly in the fields, planting and harvesting crops. Their work supported the Spartan citizens.

HELOTS AND PERIOECI

Spartan society was divided into three main social classes: Spartans, helots, and perioeci. Spartans, also called Spartiates, were full citizens of the state. This group could trace their family history all the way back to the original inhabitants of Sparta. Spartiates were the only group allowed to vote and take part in politics. To become a full citizen, you must have completed the agoge, the Spartan military training program. As a result, Spartiates were also Sparta's standing army, and completely devoted themselves to military training and service. They were not allowed to take part in manual labor. That was the place of the helot, or slave class.

Helots were descended from the conquered people of Messinia and Lakonia, around Sparta. They were owned by the state. Helots took care of everyday tasks like farming, which allowed the Spartans the time needed to become the only full-time army in all of Greece. Though there were many more helots than Spartans, they were often treated terribly, and were sometimes killed outright, to keep them in line.

Between these two classes were the perioeci. Neither full citizens nor slaves, they often worked as traders between Sparta and other cities, or as skilled craftsmen. In fact, because Spartans were banned from anything that wasn't training or fighting, the perioeci were the ones that made all of their armor and weapons.

The perioeci were free, but they were not full citizens. They were required to supply men to fight in the Spartan army.

BEGINNING AT BIRTH

Even Spartan babies were subject to the state's rigid expectations. Shortly after birth, every child was examined. If it was not found to be up to Spartan standards, it would be abandoned, usually on a hillside. There it would die of starvation or exposure. This was not considered murder, as Greeks believed that by abandoning a baby, there was always a chance it would be found and adopted, either by a kindly stranger, or even possibly by one of the gods. This was an important distinction, as Greeks considered human sacrifice of any kind to be a terrible thing. Babies were also commonly bathed in wine instead of water, as it was believed this would toughen them up. From the moment they were born, every Spartan was raised to be as strong as possible, to better serve the state.

EDUCATION, ARTS, AND CULTURE

Both boys and girls received an education in Sparta. In the agoge, boys were both physically and mentally conditioned to become ideal soldiers. Through exercise and training, they worked toward physical perfection. They also learned military tactics and maneuvers. The virtues of courage, self-discipline, and loyalty (especially to the state) were drilled into their minds. They learned to read and write, so they could read maps on the battlefield.

Girls were taught poetry, dance, and singing, but their education also had a lot in common with that of their brothers. Physical fitness was prized in Sparta, and as a result, girls were trained to have exceptionally healthy and developed bodies.

Though this was done with boys to prepare them for battle, for girls it was to prepare them for childbirth. Sports were also a major part of both curriculums, specifically to help develop them physically.

Because of its overwhelming focus on military life, Sparta was not as well known for its art as other Greek states, especially Athens. Painted vases, bronze metalwork, and sculptures are the most common examples of Spartan art surviving today. Because Spartans were forbidden from any jobs other than soldier, most art produced in the Spartan region was actually made by the perioeci.

SPARTA'S GODS AND WORSHIP

Religion was taken very seriously in Sparta. Spartans believed in the Twelve Olympians, which were the major gods worshipped throughout all of Greece. Though not everyone agrees exactly which gods were among the twelve, Zeus, the king of the gods, was widely known to be their leader. There was also his wife, Hera, his daughter, Athena, goddess of wisdom, and his son, Ares, the god of war, who all lived on Mount Olympus.

FROM GREECE TO ROME

The Greeks and the **Romans** worshipped the same gods! However, the Romans changed all their names. So, for example, while the Greeks knew the god of war as Ares, the Romans called him Mars!

Each god had their own domains, or things they were in charge of. As a result, different gods were prayed or sacrificed to for different reasons.

Statues of Greek gods were displayed in all the city-states of ancient Greece. All Greeks believed in the same gods.

For example, if you wished to win an important battle, you might make a sacrifice to Ares, as war and violence were his domain. If you had to make a difficult voyage by boat, you might pray to Poseidon, god of the sea.

Another important figure in Spartan mythology was the hero Heracles, son of Zeus. Though not a god, he was revered, and both royal families of Sparta traced their ancestries all the way back to him.

Heracles, also known as Hercules, was a great hero in Greek mythology. He was seen as incredibly courageous and strong.

SPORTS AND ATHLETES

Spartans placed great importance on developing their bodies to the highest degree possible, and sports and athletics were encouraged. Part of every Spartan's education, regardless of gender, included training in various sports. Popular activities included running, boxing, and wrestling, as well as discus and javelin throwing.

In most of Greece, women rarely took part in sports. As a result, visitors to Sparta were amazed at how physically active the girls there were. Though the boys exercised to prepare themselves for battle, girls were encouraged to train to make their bodies strong for childbirth.

The hoplitodromos was a short foot race. Participants ran wearing military shields, helmets, and armor to show their strength.

COMPETING NAKED

In the early days of the Olympics, athletes participated in events wearing a loincloth around their waists. This item of clothing was eventually discarded, and athletes began competing nude. Partly this was due to the beautiful weather the Olympics usually enjoyed. It was also because one of the aims of the Olympics was to celebrate the beauty of the human body and what it was capable of. This nude style of competition suited the Spartans just fine, since in Sparta, everyone, man or woman, exercised naked!

Sparta was an eager participant in the ancient Olympic games. The original **Olympics** were very different from the games that take place today. For one thing, it was only open to Greek citizens, and only men competed. The events were also much more limited in number. Different kinds of foot races were very popular. There was even an event called the hoplitodromos, where competitors wore armor and shields as hoplites would in battle. This demonstrated the skills and competence a soldier would need in battle. The pentathlon was another popular event that consisted of five separate activities: wrestling, a foot trace, long jump, discus toss, and javelin throwing. A real full-body workout!

Though women weren't technically allowed to participate in the Olympics, they were allowed to enter teams of horses for the chariot races. Cynisca, a Spartan princess, did exactly that, and when the team she owned won, she was listed as the winner of the event. This made her the first female Olympic victor in history.

CHAPTER 5

BATTLE OF LEUCTRA— SPARTA'S DOWNFALL

Although its victory in the Peloponnesian War made Sparta the most powerful city-state in all of ancient Greece, its dominance did not last long. By 371 B.C., Sparta was unhappy with the city of Thebes. The city was trying to reestablish the Boetian Confederacy, an alliance similar to the Peloponnesian League, but in central Greece. When the Boetian Confederacy refused to disband, Sparta declared war.

The Spartan king Cleombrotus marched on Thebes with a force of at least 10,000 men, made up of Spartans and their allies. They met the Boetian army on the plain of Leuctra, close to Thebes. The Boetian army was led by a general named Epaminondas, who was a tactical genius. Although Sparta was famous for its strength and ability on the battlefield, Epaminondas convinced the Boetians not to run from the attack, even though they had a smaller force, between 7,000 to 9,000 troops.

During the Battle of Leuctra, Epaminondas focused most of his strength on the left side of his force, which was unusual. Most armies concentrated their best warriors on their right. Epaminondas lined up his infantry fifty men deep on his left wing, much deeper than the normal twelve. He also advanced them ahead of the rest of his force.

Epaminondas transformed the ancient Greek city of Thebes by conquering the Spartan army. He was killed by a spear in a later battle with the Spartans. Following Greek custom, he was buried on the battlefield.

Unused to these new tactics, the Spartans were unsure how to react. The Boetians made short work of them, killing the Spartan king and slaughtering at least 1,000 members of his army.

This defeat shattered Sparta's control of Greece. After generations of belief that Sparta was an unstoppable military **juggernaut**, Thebes showed that they could be beaten. After just 35 years of rule, Sparta was overthrown. Thebes became the dominant power in Greece, and shortly afterwards the helots would gain their freedom. Much like Athens after the Peloponnesian War, Sparta became a shell of what it once was. Sparta would never again reach the heights of power or influence it had known.

Modern-day Sparta is located on the site of ancient Sparta. Outside of the city, you can find the ruins of an ancient Spartan theater next to the vast olive groves.

Today, Sparta has about 18,000 inhabitants. It is famous for its olives and citrus processing.

Even though its rule was fairly short, the legend of Sparta lives on. Throughout the ages, it has been used as an ideal example of what can be achieved when a goal is completely committed to body, mind, and soul.

Today, the city of Sparta, called Sparti in modern Greek, exists where the ancient city once did. The modern version of the city was founded in 1834 by King Otto, the ruler of Greece at the time. It's home to many museums, including one just about olives and olive oil! It's also the capital of modern-day Laconia.

GLOSSARY

alliance: a formal agreement between two or more regions or nations

city-state: a city that also has other areas outside of itself that depend on it

democracy: a form of government where people choose leaders by voting

Greece: a country in the southeast part of Europe

hoplite: a foot soldier in ancient Greece, they typically wore armor and carried spears and shields

infantry: foot soldiers, soldiers who fight on the ground

juggernaut: a massive force that overpowers and destroys anything in its path

military: an organized group of soldiers who protect and fight for the interests of a city, state, or country

Neolithic: an era in prehistoric times when farming was widely adopted by humanity, ending by 2,000 B.C.

Olympics: a series of sports competitions, begun in ancient Greece

peninsula: a piece of land with water on three sides, but that is still connected to a larger landmass

Persian Empire: an ancient dynasty based in what is today known as Iran

Romans: people from ancient Rome, an empire in what is now known as Italy

FOR MORE INFORMATION

Books

Charles River Editors. *A History of Ancient Athens and Sparta for Children.*
Cambridge, MA: Charles River Editors, 2013.

DiPrimio, Pete. *Ancient Sparta.*
Newark, DE: Mitchell Lane Publishers, 2012.

McLeese, Don. *Spartans.*
Vero Beach, FL: Rourke Publishing, 2011.

Sepahban, Lois. *Spartan Warriors.*
North Mankato, MN: Child's World, 2015.

Websites

Due to the changing nature of Internet links, PowerKids Press has developed an online list of websites related to the subject of this book. This site is updated regularly. Please use this link to access the list:

www.powerkidslinks.com/acc/sparta

INDEX